D0929759

Everything You Need to Know About

LIVING IN A
SHELTER

Homelessness is especially difficult for teens.

• THE NEED TO KNOW LIBRARY •

Everything You Need to Know About

LIVING IN A SHELTER

Julie Parker

THE ROSEN PUBLISHING GROUP, INC.
NEW YORK

Published in 1995 by The Rosen Publishing Group, Inc.
29 East 21st Street, New York, NY 10010

First Edition

Manufactured in the United States of America

Library of Congress Cataloging-in-Publication Data

Parker, Julie F.
    Everything you need to know about living in a shelter / Julie
Parker.
        p.   cm. — (The need to know library)
    Includes bibliographical references and index.
    ISBN 0-8239-1874-2
    1. Shelters for the homeless—United States—Juvenile literature.
2. Homeless children—Housing—United States—Juvenile literature.
[1. Shelters for the homeless.   2. Homeless persons.]   I. Title.
II. Series.
HV4505.P27   1995
362.5—dc20   94-21280
                                                                    CIP
                                                                    AC

Contents

Introduction

If you are a teenager living without a home, you're not alone. Today there are more homeless people in the United States than at any time since the Great Depression in the 1920s and '30s. Although being homeless is difficult for anyone, it is toughest on young people who may not be ready or able to take care of themselves. If you are a homeless teenager, you may feel as if no one can understand what you are going through. Yet many people are working to help you, and you can usually find help at a shelter.

Finding out the number of homeless children and teens in the U.S. is difficult. Estimates range from the tens of thousands to a million, with 500,000 a figure that many researchers accept. Each one of these young people has his or her own story about becoming homeless. But all of them would rather have a safe home so that each day was not such a struggle.

As they get through each day, homeless teens survive in many kinds of environments, either by themselves or with their families. Some live with friends or relatives for a period of time, often in crowded conditions. Others seek shelter in a building that is abandoned or condemned as unsafe. Some go to campgrounds and try to make a temporary home there. Some live in their cars or fend for themselves on the street, while others live in welfare hotels. Many turn to shelters for lodging and help. Each setting has its own problems and challenges.

Homeless people have reached their situations in various ways. Maybe a family never had a home because they lacked money. The loss of a job or the sale of an apartment building may cause a family to become homeless. Maybe a fire destroyed a house or an apartment. Perhaps a family split up, leaving some members out. Natural disasters such as floods or earthquakes can leave many people suddenly homeless. Sometimes teenagers run away from abuse at home or are thrown out because of family fights. Living without a home can force a teenager to fend for herself or himself.

Sam has never really had a place he called home. His mother was 16 when he was born, and she was kicked out by her parents. All he remembers of his early years was moving around a lot and waking up out of nightmares not knowing where he was. Now Sam is 15 and has three younger sisters. His mother and sisters live in a family shelter, but Sam cannot be with them. Since he is male and over 12 years old, the rules will not let him sleep there overnight. He has no real friends because he has never stayed in one place long enough to make them. Sam is now living with his fourth foster family. He still wakes up sometimes with the same nightmares.

Emily is from the country and finds it hard to believe how her life changed so quickly. She used to live with her sister and her parents in a three-bedroom colonial house on their farm. But the floods destroyed all that. The river half a mile away overran their home and ruined the land. Although they had some insurance, it wasn't enough to start over. So the family moved to another state to live with Emily's grandmother. Now the whole family has to share one room, and everyone is always fighting. Emily wishes that she could go back to her old school and her friends and be in her own room with her own clothes. But her room and her clothes are gone, and she doesn't know if the family will ever have a home.

Kristen ran away from home because of her mother's boyfriend. Her parents were divorced when she was three years old, and ever since her mother has invited a series of boyfriends to live with them. Often while she was growing up, Kristen felt as if she were the mother, because she took care of the cleaning, shopping, and cooking. In school she was a good student and pretended that everything was fine

Teens are sometimes forced to deal with situations they did not create.

at home. But late one night her mother's latest boyfriend came into her room. Before Kristen knew what was happening, he ripped off her nightgown and raped her. The next morning Kristen got out the money she had saved from baby-sitting. Instead of going to school, she took a bus to the city. She wasn't sure what she would do or where she would go. She just knew that she had to get far away.

These three teenagers are homeless for very different reasons, but they all have one thing in common. They have no home because of a crisis that they did not *cause*. Sam obviously did not cause his mother to get pregnant or his grand-

People are often left homeless because of circumstances beyond their control, such as flooding or other natural disasters.

parents to make her leave their house. Emily had nothing to do with creating the flood that took her home. Kristen did not choose to have this man live with her and her mother, and no one but the rapist is responsible for rape. If our society were different, there would be more places where people who lose one home could go to find another. But sadly, most people are homeless simply because there is not enough affordable housing. For young people, the situation is very unfair; they did not cause the problem, but still they have to deal with it.

In coping with homelessness, a teen might turn

to a shelter. Long-term solutions are complicated and require such things as low-priced housing, job training, better education, and lots of money from government and private sources. But for now, if you are homeless, changes in society are not your immediate concern. As you focus on getting through one day at a time, a shelter might provide some help.

Thousands of homeless people need shelter in our cities.

Chapter 1

Life in a Shelter

Like homes, shelters come in all shapes and sizes. What it is like to live in a shelter depends to a great extent on that particular shelter. Some shelters are set up with small beds in a large room of a school or church, just to provide a place to sleep for the night. Sometimes houses are taken over by an agency that helps the homeless. Temporary shelters are made of tents, and cots are brought in by the Red Cross or another relief organization to help people who have suffered from a natural disaster. Other facilities are built specifically as shelters, designed to meet the needs of the homeless.

Shelters offer a warm place to rest at night. Some provide meals or can tell you where you can get food. The community may have soup kitchens that offer hot meals or a food pantry that supplies bags of groceries. Temporary shelters set up after a natural disaster may offer medical care for people who have been injured. But all shelters are meant to be short-term housing, so it can be hard to find the comforts of home.

Even the simple parts of a daily routine can be difficult when you are living in a shelter. There may be no place to shower. The times when you can take a shower may be limited, or there may not be enough hot water. Without enough to eat, you may go through the day hungry. Perhaps you have no place to cook and find it hard to have a balanced diet on fast food. If the shelter provides food, you may have no choice of what or when you will eat. There may be no phone you can use, or if there is a phone it may be used by lots of people. If the shelter has rules, you need to obey them. Simple decisions like what time the lights are out and when you go to bed may not be your own.

Especially hard for teenagers is the lack of privacy. In a shelter it is very rare to have a space that you can call your own. There may be no place to keep your things, or you have to worry about their being stolen. Doing homework becomes a big challenge without a quiet place to work. Getting together with friends is hard when you can't invite them over or call them up. Every day causes stress.

Other problems come up from time to time. Infestations and diseases like lice and tuberculosis can spread rapidly where a lot of people share the

Your bed may be the only space you have to call your own in a shelter.

same living space. You or your family may not have enough money to see a doctor when someone is sick, so medical care comes from visits to the hospital emergency room. The shelter may be far from your home community and your school. If the shelter closes during the day, you may have to leave in the morning and have nowhere to go. Some people in the shelter may be mentally ill and act strangely. Fights and violence may keep you on edge, or worse, hurt you. Certain shelters are so scary that some homeless people prefer to take their chances on the street.

Those who do stay in shelters learn to make the best of where they are. If stealing is common, they sometimes sleep with their shoes on and use their clothes as a pillow. Especially in larger shelters, it could be helpful to stay near the security guards or other shelter workers. Avoiding involvement in fights is also smart. Some people sleep during the day so they can be more alert at night when it is more dangerous. By keeping your wits about you and thinking clearly, you can help yourself cope with life in a shelter.

Chapter 2

Coping with Feelings

Your teenage years are hard enough, even without being homeless. They are a time when your body is changing and you are discovering new emotional and sexual feelings. Peer pressure is strong to fit in, to dress and act in certain ways. You are learning who you are and thinking about your future.

In addition to all this, if you are a homeless teenager, you may have some uncomfortable feelings. If you don't want your friends to know that you are homeless, you may be inventing stories about where you live. You may be angry at the people who are responsible for the way you are living, or frustrated because you can't change things. Perhaps you are worried about dangers. All these feelings are natural and understandable. What you do with them is up to you.

Living in a shelter means doing without a lot of things other people take for granted such as privacy and safety. You may find that your belongings occasionally disappear.

Embarrassment and Shame

If you do something or something happens to you that you do not want other people to know about, you probably feel embarrassed. When this feeling is very strong, you may be ashamed.

Marisol, 15, lives in a family shelter with her mother and younger sister. Juan is a guy in math class who really likes Marisol. Every day he leaves notes in her locker telling her how smart and pretty she is. At lunchtime he buys snacks for her and is always very polite. One day in the cafeteria Juan asks Marisol for her phone number. Although she likes him, she doesn't want him—or anyone else at school—to know that she lives in a shelter. Marisol is embarrassed. She starts giving Juan the cold shoulder so he won't like her anymore.

Anger

If you feel mad at someone or something, you are angry. You may get angry all of a sudden, or it could be a feeling that you have had for a long time. People express their anger in all sorts of ways.

Colin's father drinks a lot. Because he spent too much money on alcohol, Colin's father did not pay the rent for a few months, and the family were evicted from their apartment. The family split up, and Colin has been living with a friend for a few weeks. His father is on the street. Colin sees him sometimes on his way to school and is so mad at him that he wants to hit him. Instead, he walks by and pretends not to know his father, or he gives him a mean look. Colin is so angry that he is afraid of what he might do.

Frustration

Sometimes there are problems that you want to solve, but for some reason you cannot. You feel helpless or powerless. You may try to do something but get no results. This can make you feel frustrated.

Erin's mother was laid off when the factory where she worked closed down. She looked for work for months, as their savings ran out, but many people in the town also needed jobs, and very few were available. Erin, her two brothers, and her mother lost their home when they weren't able to pay the rent. Erin hates to see her mother feeling such a failure. She wishes that she could help her mother get a job, but there is nothing she can do. Erin feels frustrated.

Fear

If you are afraid of something, you feel fear. You may be afraid of a person. You may worry about dangers in the place where you live. When you are fearful you may become tense, or your stomach may ache. This is your body's way of telling you that you need to be careful.

Ed sleeps in a large shelter for men. His parents threw him out of the house because he is gay. Ed is 16, but he lied about his age to be let into this shelter for men eighteen and older. Ed's sneakers have been stolen. At night there are lots of fights. Ed is sure he would be picked on if the men knew that he is gay. Ed tries to act tough, but he feels fearful.

These are some of the many feelings that homeless teenagers may have. Uncomfortable

Fear and depression are feelings many homeless teenagers have.

emotions like embarrassment or shame, anger, frustration, and fear let you know that something is wrong. If you lock up these feelings inside, they can be dangerous. They can lead to depression or violence. But if you find ways to use these feelings positively, they can actually be helpful.

You need to think about what you can control and what you can't. Marisol cannot control the fact that she lives in a shelter, but she can choose what to tell Juan. She might tell Juan that she likes him but she can't get calls at home, so maybe they could make plans at school. Colin can't control the fact that his father drinks, but he might tell his guidance counselor about the situation.

Counselors can help you sort through your feelings and suggest resources where you might find more help. (There is also a list of places where you could go for help at the end of this book.) The guidance counselor could tell Colin about Alateen, a support group for teenagers who have an alcoholic in the family. Erin might tell another adult she trusts about her mother's unemployment. Or at least she could write her feelings in a journal so she would not feel alone. Ed might talk with a worker at the shelter. He might decide to work things through with his parents, or he might try to find a relative he could stay with while he goes back to school. Either way, talking things through with a trustworthy person who cares about you could help to make you feel better.

Chapter 3

Problems You May Face

Because life in a shelter can be so upsetting, teenagers find different ways to deal with the stress. Some of these ways could hurt you seriously. It can be very tempting to try to forget your problems by using drugs or alcohol. Some teenagers join a gang to feel as if they belong somewhere. Gangs are often violent and steal or vandalize things for fun. Some teenagers take out their anger by attacking other people physically or sexually. To get money, some teenagers sell their bodies for sex. It may seem that these activities meet a need for belonging or getting money or getting even, but they are not worth the risk.

Randy's father died two years ago, and ever since his family has been much poorer. Randy lives in a family shelter with his mother and brother and feels sad a lot of the time. One Friday night Randy went to a party at a friend's house. There was a keg of beer, and Randy tried it. He thought it tasted awful, but he pretended that he liked it in front of his friends. After a couple of drinks, it didn't taste so bad. For a little while, he forgot his problems. Randy started looking for ways to drink more often. Early in the morning he would sneak a drink before going to school, then brush his teeth so his breath wouldn't smell of alcohol. He stopped caring about school and cut classes to drink with other kids in the parking lot behind the schoolyard. All he wanted to do was drink.

Bill lives in a welfare hotel with his mother, who feels stressed all the time and yells at him constantly. Bill hates this and stays away from her as much as he can. Down the block from the hotel he sees a group of boys who are in a gang called The Kicks. They wear black jackets, expensive basketball sneakers, and jeans with a chain instead of a belt. One of the guys in the gang, Joe, lives in the hotel also, and Bill starts hanging out with him. Joe offers to help Bill get into The Kicks, but there are things that Bill has to do first. To join the gang he has to mug someone, and he has to carry a "piece" or gun. Bill wonders if this is the right thing to do, but the Kicks seem so cool and he really wants to belong.

After Kristen was raped by her mother's boyfriend, she ran away to the city. She passed the days

Fighting or other violent behavior is often a result of stress or frustration.

walking around and trying to find a place to keep warm. Soon she had spent the little money she had on food. The first three nights Kristen slept in the bus station and pretended that she was waiting for a bus. The fourth night the police made her move. Kristen was scared and hungry. As she roamed the streets trying to think of where she could go, she saw a girl about her age standing in a doorway. The girl, Robin, called her over and asked if she wanted to make good money. Robin was a prostitute and knew that her pimp would be pleased if she found a new girl. Robin told Kristen that all she would have to do was lie down and think of something else. In return she would be protected, have food, money, clothes,

Using drugs and alcohol will only make your problems worse.

and a place to live. Kristen decided to try "turning tricks." The way Robin put it, it didn't sound so bad. Besides, she was hungry.

Randy, Bill, and Kristen are headed for big trouble. They are breaking the law and hurting themselves. They could end up injured, in prison, or dead.

Abusing Drugs and Alcohol

Randy's drinking may not seem like a big deal, but he is using a drug. Some drugs are helpful and are prescribed by a doctor. Drugs such as pot, crack, cocaine, heroin, angel dust, and LSD are illegal. Some of them, like crack and heroin, are highly addictive. Your body craves more and more of the drug. Alcohol is a legal drug for people over 21, but it can still be very dangerous. You can also become addicted to alcohol over time. Once you are hooked, breaking the habit of using any drug is very hard. Your body goes through withdrawal, and you feel sick without the drug. Even if your drug is alcohol, you become a drug addict.

Joining Gangs

Bill's joining the gang is also dangerous. Some gangs are not harmful, but others are very violent. To get into a gang you must do things that may involve hurting others or yourself. Some gangs, called posses, deal drugs. Gangs have strict rules. Some people must be your instant enemies. Gang members often carry weapons. Sometimes they "go wilding," setting out to attack, rape, steal, and even murder. People in gangs often do things that they would not do on their own. But when they are caught, they can find themselves alone.

Selling Yourself

Kristen also will find herself alone as a prostitute. Although the pimp says that he will take care of her, he really just uses her to make money. As a prostitute, Kristen loses control over her life. Movies and television may show teenage prostitutes as glamorous, but in real life selling your body is awful. Many prostitutes start taking drugs to forget what they are doing. Then they become addicted to the drug and need money to pay for it. It becomes hard to break out of the cycle.

Sexually Transmitted Diseases

People who have sex with different partners, whether they are prostitutes or not, run the risk of contracting a sexually transmitted disease (STD). Gonorrhea and chlamydia are painful but respond to treatment. There is no cure for herpes, a painful disease. There is, as yet, no cure for AIDS (acquired immunodeficiency syndrome), which is fatal. The best way to avoid these serious diseases is to practice abstinence until marriage—do not have sex until you are married. The next best way is to practice safer sex, using a condom. Not using a condom can result not only in an STD, but in pregnancy as well.

Breaking the Law

Randy, Bill, and Kristen could damage their lives in other ways. Underage drinking, mugging people, and prostituting yourself are against the law. People rarely are arrested for underage

Breaking the law by using illegal drugs may get you
arrested.

drinking, but they do get arrested for related
crimes such as driving drunk. If you are caught
doing something illegal, you will be charged with
the crime and taken to court. If you arc found
guilty, you will be sentenced by a judge. You might
end up in a juvenile detention center or in jail,
depending on your age and any previous record.
In correctional facilities such as jail, there are new
rules and tough ways to survive. Being locked up
is frightening.

You may be young, but the law still applies to
you, and the punishment will too. If you do receive
a sentence, the rest of your life becomes harder
because you have a criminal record. Think about

There are people you can turn to for help.

what might happen before you do something illegal.

Taking Control of Yourself

Randy, Bill, and Kristen have tough lives. They did not start out with the advantages of a healthy family that could give them the emotional and financial support they need. Still, they do have some control over what happens to them. Even in difficult situations, they can try to make smart decisions and find ways to help themselves. People and organizations are there to help, but you need to take the first step and seek them out.

Chapter 4

What You Can Do for Yourself

Homeless teens face lots of problems, but they can be overcome—with a lot of hard work and effort. Determination is very important. The fact that you are reading this book shows that you care enough to want to make your life better. If you are motivated enough to give yourself a bright future, chances are very good that you can get the help you need, set goals for yourself, work toward them, and succeed.

Get an Education

When Emily's family lost their home in a flood, they moved to her grandmother's house. Since her parents did not know where they would go next, they decided to enroll Emily and her sister in school there. At first Emily was angry about having to go to

Going to a new school is difficult under any circumstances.

a new school away from her friends, but after a while she decided to make the best of it. Anyway, she liked school more than her grandmother's house; there everyone was in each other's way all the time. Emily stayed after school in the library to do her homework. Because she studied so much, Emily got three As on her report card. Her parents were proud of her. Even some of the kids in her classes started noticing that this new girl was smart. Emily realized that even though many things were wrong right now, studying was something that made people notice her in a good way.

Like Emily, most of the people who like school are the people who do well. If you want to get good grades, you need to spend time studying. Even if you have no home, perhaps you can find places to do homework at school or at the library. Maybe you could study during a free period. If you don't understand an assignment, ask the teacher or someone else in the class for help. Teachers like to see that their students are trying.

Some students drop out of school because of pregnancy. If you are a young woman who becomes pregnant, you need to be aware of the choices facing you. If it is early enough in your pregnancy, you could choose to have an abortion. You might decide to keep the baby or put the baby up for adoption. These are serious decisions that you need to make with the father of the baby and the help of adults whom you trust. If you decide to become a parent, you might find out whether your school district offers special classes for pregnant teenagers.

A good education helps you follow the path to success. It can be difficult for homeless teens, however, especially if they move a lot or live far from their school. Some of them stop caring about school and cut classes because they consider them a waste of time. But without a high school education you will be cut off from many opportunities. School also teaches skills that you need for the rest of your life. Reading and writing are necessary even to fill out a job application. It is very important to stay in school.

Your school may also offer job training programs. Teenagers who do not want or are not able to go to college can gain valuable skills that prepare them for a career in various fields. If you like working with machines, you might be a good mechanic. If you are interested in personal care or office work or computers, you might want to become a beautician or a secretary or a word processor. These careers can offer good salaries, but they require training. Many school districts have programs for students who want to learn a vocational skill, but you need to be in school to take advantage of them. Your guidance counselor can tell you what is available in your school district.

It can be difficult to concentrate on school when your life has been turned upside down, but it will be worth the effort.

Participating in sports or another activity or hobby can help relieve
stress and give you a solid sense of accomplishment.

Develop Your Talents and Abilities

Sam has spent most of his life living with different foster families, but he is determined to stay with this one. That is not so much because of the foster parents, who are okay, but because of the basketball coach at his current school. Sam is a talented basketball player and always plays first-string. This year the team is doing really well and may go on to the championships. The coach thinks that Sam could get a basketball scholarship to college. Sam needs to work hard at his classes to graduate, but he likes the idea of going to college. Then he could keep playing basketball and get a college degree.

Doing things you enjoy (as long as they don't hurt anyone else) can help relieve stress and give you a sense of accomplishment. What do you like to do? What are you good at? Maybe you like sports and could play on a team. Sports like running and basketball don't need a lot of expensive equipment and are great exercise. If you like to sing, you might join a choral group in your school, church, synagogue, or some community organization. If you like to draw or paint, you might create art on your own or see if an art class is offered at school. Exploring your talents and improving your abilities can let you have fun, gain skills, and feel good about yourself.

A teacher or counselor might be able to help you find the information you need.

Learn from Experience

When Colin's family became homeless because of his father's drinking, Colin felt that he hated his dad. Colin trusted his guidance counselor at school, Ms. Pincus, and let her know about his problem. Ms. Pincus told Colin about Alateen, a support group for teenagers who come from an alcoholic families. She helped him find out about a meeting that he could attend. Colin felt funny about going, but decided to give it a try. When he got there, he was surprised how honest everyone was. At a few meetings Colin even saw Jocelyn, a very popular girl from his school; he had had no idea that she had any problems. Colin came to learn that alcoholism is a disease, and that some researchers think it is passed from one generation to the next. Although he was shocked to hear this, he was also glad to find it out. Colin decided that he was not going to abuse alcohol. There was no way he was going to risk ending up like his father.

Colin saw how addiction to alcohol had ruined his father and split the family apart. Colin hopes to have a family one day too, but he vows never to put them through this pain. While homeless teenagers may not be able to change their situation instantly, they do know what is wrong. When they become adults in charge of their own lives, they can know what *not* to do. Like Colin, some homeless teenagers see mistakes that those

Friends are often a good source of support.

around them have made and decide to learn from them.

In any problem situation, like being a homeless teenager, there are factors that you can control— and those you cannot. As you try to make your life better, decide what you can do to help yourself. You can control, at least to some extent, how hard you try to get an education, how you use your abilities, and whether you learn from experience. In the next chapter, you will see how you can also find people who might help you.

Chapter 5

Getting Help from Others

It is important that you tell your problems to someone who cares about you. It may take some searching to find someone who has your best interests at heart. A professional counselor may be your best solution.

Professional Help

When you meet with a counselor, be alert to any warning signals. If you feel uncomfortable with the way the person talks to you or touches you, listen to your feelings and get away from that person. But if you find someone who is actively on your side, you need to treat that person with respect and tell the truth. Remember that for both of you it will take time to build trust.

Talking to a counselor about what you're going through can be very helpful.

Peers

When teenagers have something to talk about, they usually turn first to their friends. Because they are so important, you need to choose your friends carefully. Do your friends like you for yourself or because of a group or gang you belong to? Do your friends want you to succeed, or do they want you to be like them even if that means cutting school or doing drugs? Are your friends happy for you when something goes well, or are they jealous? Do your friends tell you what they think directly, or do they talk about you behind

Sometimes a parent is the best person to turn to.

your back? Real friends like you for who you are and want the best for you.

But even very close friends may not have all the answers or information you need. For example, if you suddenly became homeless your best friend might take time to listen and try to make you feel better, but she or he probably would not know where you could go for help. Sometimes a friend might treat you differently for fear of becoming homeless too. That is why it is good to find an adult or two who can be there for you.

Parent(s)

Whether or not you feel that you can turn to your parent(s) depends on your relationship. Does your mother or father listen to what you have to say? Do you try to talk with them about what matters to you? If you have had a good relationship with your parent(s), they may seem to change under the stress of being homeless. Remember that most parents love their children very much, even though they have problems of their own. If you are living in a shelter with your parent(s), it might be helpful to share your feelings. If you are a teen without a parent, you might talk with a relative who has acted in a parental role for you, such as a grandparent. If you do not get along with your own parent(s), maybe the parent of a friend would be willing to help you.

Social workers are trained to help people.

Clergy

You may already know a clergyperson (minister, priest, or rabbi) from your church or synagogue. Even if you're not a member of any religious group, you should feel free to ask the ministers, rabbis, or priests in the community for help. Clergy are listed in the phone book under "Community Listings" or in the yellow pages under "Churches" and "Synagogues." Most clergy are aware of the resources in their community and may be able to make phone calls for you or help you get the services you need.

Social Workers

Social workers are trained to help people work through their problems. Some social workers have jobs at shelters to help clients find homes. Schools usually have a social worker to help students with problems. If you know a social worker, she or he could work with you to find the services and programs that are right for you.

Guidance Counselors

Schools employ guidance counselors to help students make the most of their school years. Guidance counselors are also trained to advise people and help them consider steps beyond graduation. If your living situation is affecting your school work, you might share this concern with your guidance counselor. She or he may have suggestions about programs offered by the school or other resources in the community that could assist you.

Teachers

You may have a teacher who could help you. Many teens with problems turn to a certain teacher whom they know and like. Although your teacher may not know of programs that can help you, she or he might be able to put you in touch with someone who can. At least, a concerned teacher can listen to you so you don't keep your feelings bottled up inside.

Librarians

The library can put you in touch with the resources you need. The reference librarian usually has a file of community resources. Some libraries have community service specialists trained to help people sort through their difficulties.

Shelter Staff and Volunteers

Generally, the people who work at a shelter are there because they care about the homeless. The paid staff do not make high salaries, and volunteers often do much of the work to keep the shelter going. Shelter workers would know of the options available to you, whether that be finding an apartment, entering a job training program, or staying in school. Whether they are paid staff or volunteers, those who work at a shelter are usually good people to turn to for assistance and understanding.

The very least a concerned teacher will do is listen.

More low-rent housing must be made available to people with low incomes.

Chapter 6

Changes in Society

The United States Declaration of Independence states that each person has the right to "life, liberty, and the pursuit of happiness." That means that everybody deserves the opportunity to live a decent life. For the growing number of people who have had their home destroyed or taken away or who never had a home, their basic needs are increasingly not being met. To reverse this alarming trend, major changes in society must take place.

The most obvious change needed is the building of more decent, affordable housing. Much of the low-income housing that exists is in dangerous neighborhoods with poor-quality schools. The housing allowances provided by social service agencies usually are not adequate to cover a living space for a good-sized family. More low-rent housing must be made available for people who cannot afford to buy a home. Support and

Public schools sometimes offer programs or guidance for teens who do not plan to go on to college.

expansion are needed for organizations like Habitat for Humanity, which help poor people build houses that they then own. Zoning codes that specify what can be built where need to be adjusted so that neighborhoods are more integrated, instead of separating people by their level of income. Communities need to be safe for all the people who live there.

People also need good jobs and the skills to fulfill them. Public school systems should offer more options for those who decide not to go to college. Job and educational training programs that pay fair wages should be available to help people earn their own living. Parents, especially those who are young, should have easy access to parenting classes. Working parents of young children must be able to find affordable child care. People who receive hourly wages should be able to earn enough to support themselves, with health-care coverage and job stability. Reform of the welfare system and the health-care system are also important.

These changes will require considerable attention and money, as well as many years of commitment. Right now some organizations are working for long-term improvements in how our country cares for the homeless. You can ask them for more information.

National Coalition for the Homeless
1612 K Street NW
Washington, DC 20006
(202) 775-1322

National Low Income Housing Coalition/
    Organization
1012 14th Street, NW
Washington, DC 20005
(202) 662-1530

We still have a long way to go in helping people who are living without a home, but there is growing public awareness of this widespread problem. Some people are homeless because of

Ultimately, everybody can control how they react to any situation they may find themselves in. It is up to you to make the most of your opportunities in life.

bad choices they have made, but many others are homeless because of events beyond their control. This is usually true of homeless teenagers. But if you are a homeless teenager, you *can* control what you do now. You can take charge of finding ways to help yourself. While living in a shelter today, you can find hope for a better tomorrow.

Glossary

abortion Medical procedure that ends a pregnancy.

abuse To use something or someone wrongly.

addict One who is dependent on alcohol or another drug.

adoption The process of giving a baby to parents other than the natural parents.

AIDS (acquired immunodeficiency syndrome) Fatal disease in which the body's immune system breaks down.

alcohol Substance that affects the body chemically and makes one think less clearly.

chlamydia A sexually transmitted disease.

correctional facility Place where people who are charged with a crime may be held before trial or be punished for breaking the law.

crack Form of cocaine that can be smoked.

depression Extreme sadness.

gang Group of people who claim an area (or turf) and enforce strict rules on members.

gonorrhea A sexually transmitted disease.

heroin Addictive drug made from morphine.

juvenile detention center Place where young people who are charged with a crime may be held before trial or be punished for breaking the law.

lice Small insects that infest hair and skin covered by hair.

pimp Person who finds customers for prostitutes and who receives part of their earnings.

prostitute Someone who has sex for money.

rape Any forced act of sexual intercourse.

tuberculosis (TB) Serious disease of the lungs that is spread easily (usually by coughing).

violence Use of physical force to injure someone or something.

volunteer Someone who works without getting paid.

welfare hotel Place where homeless people stay for a fee paid by the government.

withdrawal Process of breaking dependence on an addictive drug.

Where to Get Help

To find organizations that can help you, a good place to begin is your phone book. Under Community Services or Social Services, you will find numbers to call for shelter and services for the homeless. There will also be numbers for runaways and victims of domestic violence, rape, and child abuse. Phone numbers for emergency services are answered 24 hours a day, and hotlines often have toll-free 800 numbers. If the number is not toll-free, you can usually call collect.

When you call a hotline, a trained person answers who is there to listen to you and try to help. Everything you say is kept confidential, and you do not need to give your name.

AIDS

Public Health Service National AIDS Hotline
1-800-342-AIDS

Hetrick-Martin Institute, Inc.
Serving Gay and Lesbian Youth
401 West Street
New York, NY 10014
(212) 674-2400

ALCOHOL and DRUG ABUSE
Al-Anon Family Group Headquarters
PO Box 182, Midtown Station
New York, NY 10018
1-800 356-9996

Alcoholics Anonymous
General Service Office
PO Box 459, Grand Central Station
New York, NY 10163
(212) 870-3400

Alcohol Helpline
1-800-ALCOHOL

Center for Substance Abuse Treatment
National Drug Information, Treatment, and
    Referral Hotline
English—1-800-662-HELP
Spanish—1-800-662-9832
Hearing Impaired—1-800-228-0427

National Clearinghouse for Alcohol and Drug
    Information
PO Box 2345
Rockville, MD 20847-2345
1-800-729-6686

PREGNANCY
  National Council for Adoption
  1930 17th Street NW
  Washington, DC 20009
  (202) 328-8072 (will accept collect calls)

  Planned Parenthood Federation of America
  810 Seventh Avenue
  New York, NY 10019
  1-800-230-PLAN
  1-800-230-7526

RUNAWAYS
  National Runaway Switchboard
  1-800-621-4000

  Covenant House
  1-800-999-9999

SEXUAL ABUSE
  Childhelp USA
  1-800-4-A-CHILD
  1-800-422-4453

  Pennsylvania Coalition Against Rape
  1-800-692-7445 (9 a.m. to 5 p.m. Eastern
      Standard Time)

VARIOUS PROBLEMS
  Boystown Hotline
  1-800-448-3000

For Further Reading

Johnson, Joan J. *Kids Without Homes*. New York:
    Franklin Watts, 1991.
Kozol, Jonathan. *Rachel and Her Children*. New
    York: Ballantine, 1988.
Kryder-Coe, Julee H., Salamon, Lester M., and
    Molnar, Janice, M. (eds.). *Homeless Children
    and Youth: A New American Dilemma*. New
    Brunswick, NJ: Transaction, 1992.
Licata, Renora. *Everything You Need to Know About
    Anger*, rev.ed. New York: Rosen, 1994.
Stark, Evan, rev.ed. *Everything You Need to Know
    About Street Gangs*. New York: Rosen, 1994.
Stavsky, Lois, and Mozeson, I.E., with photos by
    Robert Hirschfield. *The Place I Call Home:
    Faces and Voices of Homeless Teens*. New York:
    Shapolsky, 1990.
Taylor, Barbara. *Everything You Need to Know
    About Alcohol*, rev.ed. New York: Rosen, 1993.

Index

About the Author

Julie Parker is an ordained minister in the United Methodist Church. She has worked as a counselor, advocate, and volunteer with the homeless.

Photo Credits

Cover, pp. 2, 25, 32, 43, 44, 50 by Lauren Piperno; pp. 9, 26, 29, 36, 38 by Kim Sonsky; p. 10 © AP/Wide World Photos; p. 12 by Kitty Hsu; pp. 15, 30 by Michael Brandt; pp. 18, 21, 35, 40, 49, 52, 54 by Yung-Hee Chia; p. 46 by Marcus Shaffer.